this ordinary thursday: the songs of georgia stitt

Original cover artwork by Derek Bishop

ISBN 978-1-4234-5095-5

WILLIAMSON MUSIC®

A RODGERS AND HAMMERSTEIN COMPANY

www.williamsonmusic.com

EXCLUSIVELY DISTRIBUTED BY

HAL•LEONARD®
CORPORATION

7777 W. BLUEMOUND RD. P.O. BOX 13819 MILWAUKEE, WI 53213

In Australia Contact:
Hal Leonard Australia Pty. Ltd.
4 Lentara Court
Cheltenham, Victoria, 3192 Australia
Email: ausadmin@halleonard.com.au

Visit Hal Leonard Online at
www.halleonard.com

georgia stitt

is a composer and a lyricist. Her musicals *Big Red Sun* (winner of the Harold Arlen Award in 2005 and written with playwright John Jiler) and *The Water* (premiered at the University of Michigan in 2004 and written with collaborators Jeff Hylton and Tim Werenko) are both in development. Georgia's non-theatrical compositions include several choral pieces, *A Better Resurrection* and *The Promise of Light*, published by Walton Music, *Let Me Sing for You*, performed at The Kennedy Center, *Echo*, performed by the Women's Chorus at the University of California, Berkeley, and *De Profundis*, premiered by the International Orange Chorale in San Francisco and published by G. Schirmer. She contributed songs to the American Music Festival in Tono, Japan and served as composer-in-residence for the Tribeca Performing Arts Center in New York City. At present she is developing a musical revue with composer/lyricist David Kirshenbaum, currently titled *Sing Me a Happy Song*. In spring of 2007 she released her first album, *This Ordinary Thursday: The Songs of Georgia Stitt*, on the PS Classics label. The recording features stellar performances by such contemporary theater luminaries as Sara Ramirez, Kelli O'Hara, Faith Prince, Carolee Carmello, Susan Egan, Tituss Burgess, Keith Byron Kirk, Andrea Burns, Matthew Morrison, Will Chase, Jenn Colella, Lauren Kennedy and Cheyenne Jackson. Additionally, Georgia has written songs which are included on Susan Egan's solo albums *Coffee House* and *Winter Tracks* (LML Records) and Lauren Kennedy's album *Here and Now* (PS Classics), and she contributed two songs to the 2008 MTV movie *The American Mall*.

Also a music director, Georgia was the assistant music director for the NBC TV special "Clash of the Choirs," the on-camera vocal coach for the NBC reality TV show "Grease: You're The One That I Want," and the Production Music Coordinator for the Disney/ABC TV musical "Once Upon A Mattress" starring Tracey Ullman and Carol Burnett. On Broadway she was the assistant conductor of the 2003 *Little Shop of Horrors* revival and the associate conductor of the Encores! production of *Can-Can* starring Patti LuPone. Also on Broadway: *Avenue Q*, *Sweet Smell of Success*, *The Music Man*, *Titanic*, *Annie*, and the national tour of *Parade*. She has also served as musical director and arranger/orchestrator for *The Broadway Divas* in concerts in New York, California and Australia and was a music consultant for the feature film *The Stepford Wives*, directed by Frank Oz. In 2005 she served as an arranger for the Boston Pops Orchestra (Keith Lockhart, conductor) in their 75th Anniversary Tribute to Stephen Sondheim at Tanglewood and Boston's Symphony Hall.

© Mike Rozman

Georgia's work as an arranger, pianist, and coach can be heard on the Broadway Cares *Home for the Holidays* CD (Centaur Records) and on the cast albums of *After the Fair*, *Shine*, *Do Re Mi* and *Little Shop of Horrors*. With lyricist Marcy Heisler she wrote and recorded *Alphabet City Cycle*, a song cycle for soprano, piano and violin. Georgia received her M.F.A. in Musical Theater Writing from New York University and her B.Mus. in Music Theory and Composition from Vanderbilt University, where she graduated *magna cum laude*. She is a recipient of the ASCAP Frederick Loewe Fellowship, the Harold Arlen Award, and the Sue Brewer Award for excellence in music composition. With director John Ruocco she created THE GYM, an ongoing professional musical theater performance class. Georgia lives in New York and Los Angeles with her husband, composer/lyricist Jason Robert Brown, and their daughter Molly.

For updates on Georgia's current projects, please visit www.georgiastitt.com.

THE HOLY SECRET

Music by GEORGIA STITT
Lyrics by LEN SCHIFF

*Recorded one whole step lower

ra - tion and de - sire____ from the start, 'til the world cracked wide____ and fell a -

part.

In the be - gin - ning did we ev - er dis - a - gree? Did we

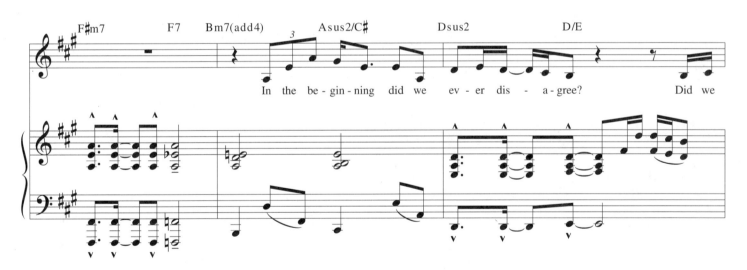

ev - er break____ the sti - fling se - ren - i - ty?____ We were

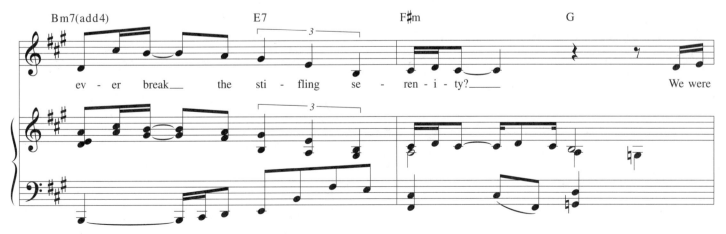

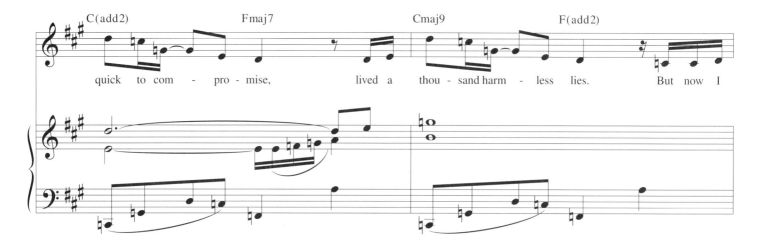

quick to com - pro - mise, lived a thou - sand harm - less lies. But now I

know: When the world cracked wide _____ it let us

go. _____

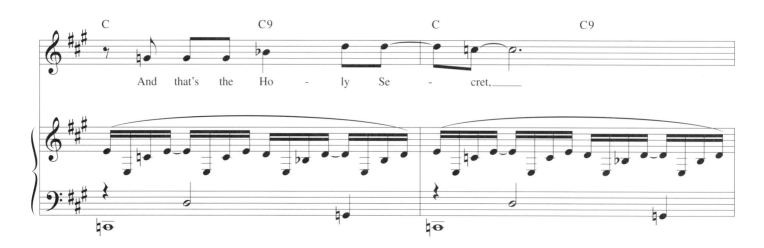

And that's the Ho - ly Se - cret, _____

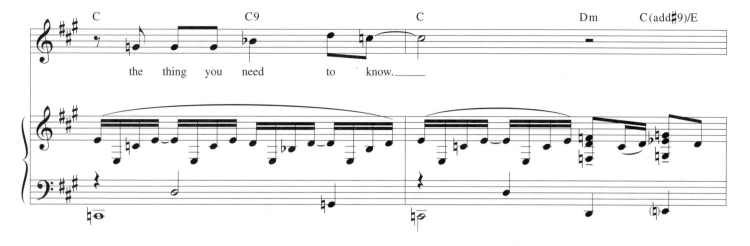

the thing you need to know.____

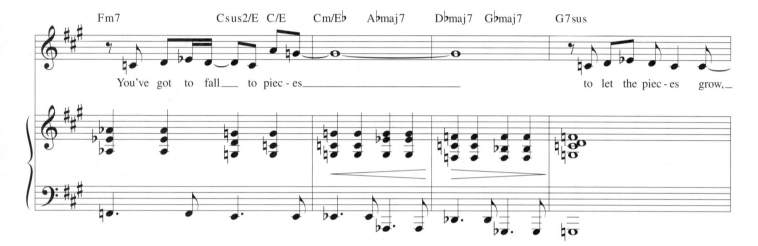

You've got to fall___ to piec-es_____ to let the piec-es grow,__

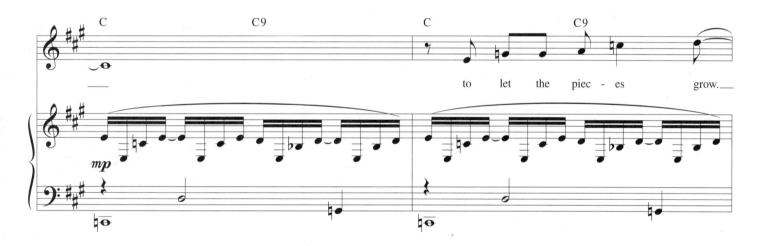

to let the piec-es grow.__

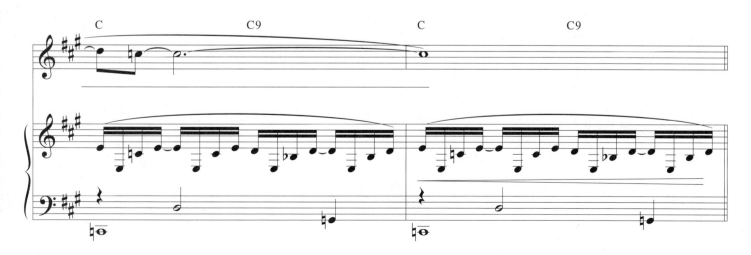

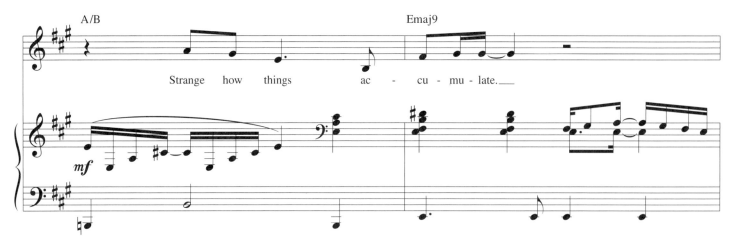

Strange how things ac - cu - mu - late.___

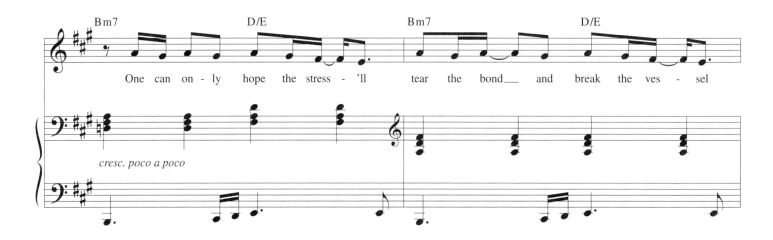

One can on - ly hope the stress - 'll tear the bond___ and break the ves - sel

be - fore the lov - ing turns to hate.___

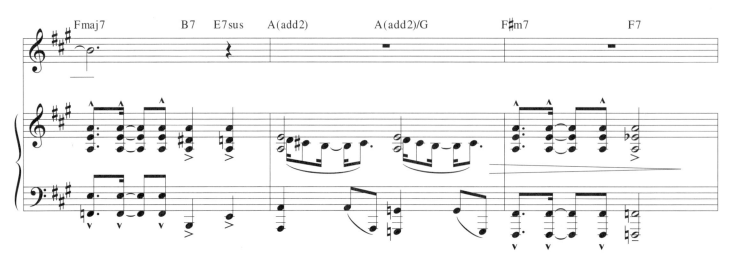

I am be-gin-ning to re-cov-er who__ I am, to dis-

cov-er what's__ a-head in the world for me.

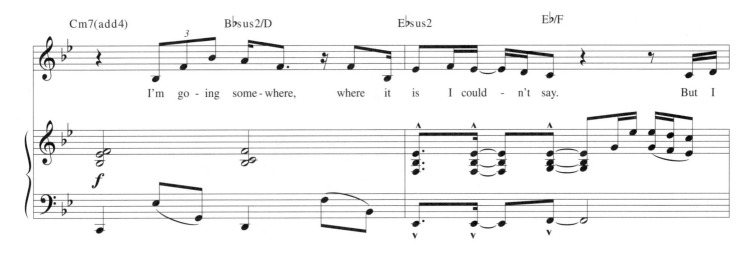

I'm go-ing some-where, where it is I could-n't say. But I

know that I'll__ be chang-ing_____ as I make my way._____ If I

feel a lit - tle sad when I think what we___ once had, it's not a sin.

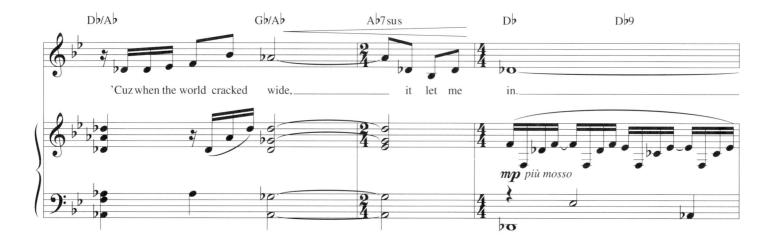

'Cuz when the world cracked wide,___ it let me in.

And that's the Ho - ly Se - cret,___

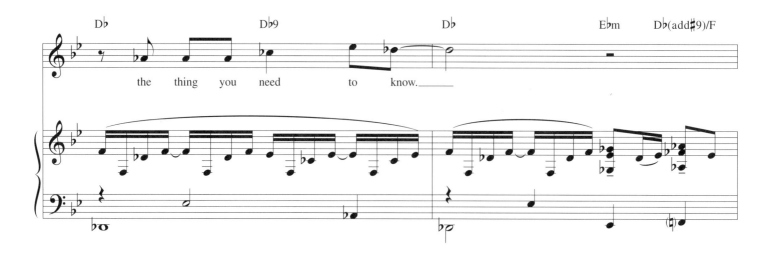

the thing you need to know.___

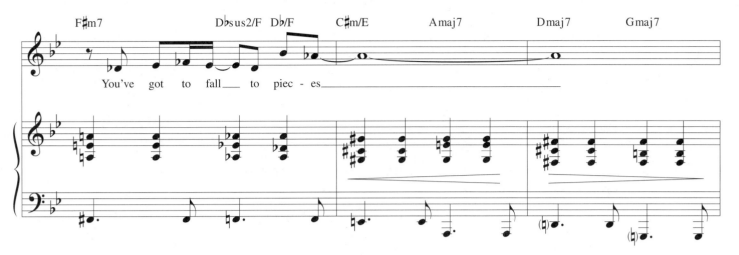

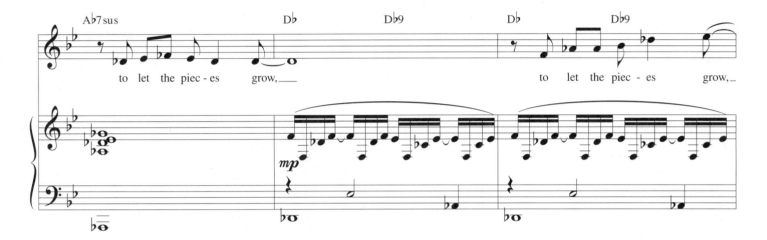

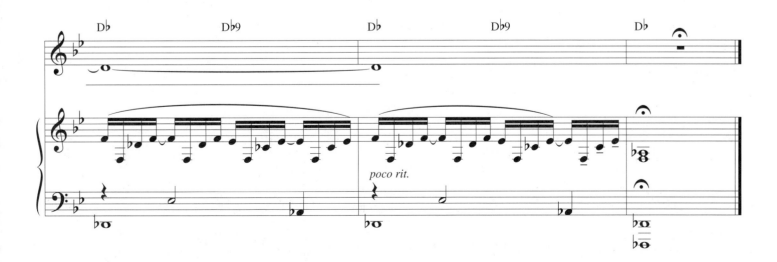

ONE DAY MORE

Music and Lyrics by
GEORGIA STITT

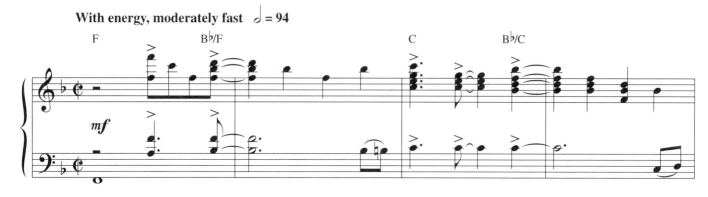

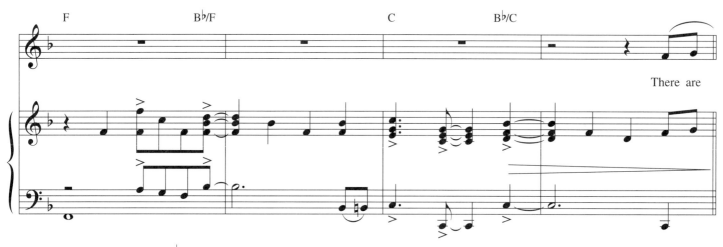

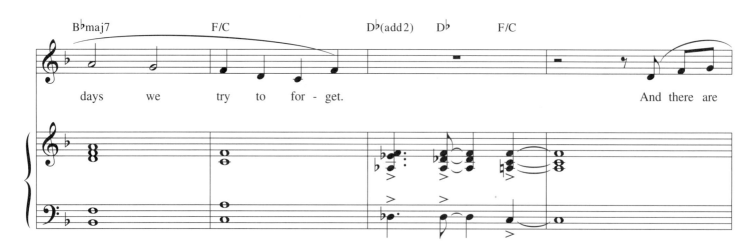

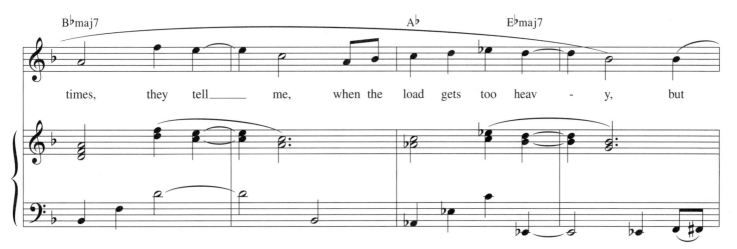

times, they tell___ me, when the load gets too heav - y, but

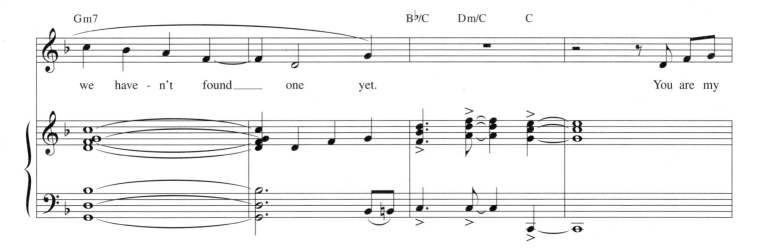

we have - n't found___ one yet. You are my

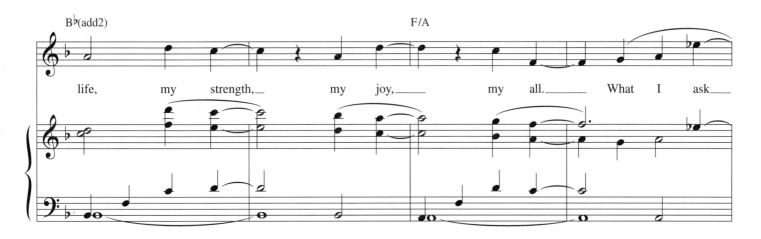

life, my strength,___ my joy,___ my all.___ What I ask___

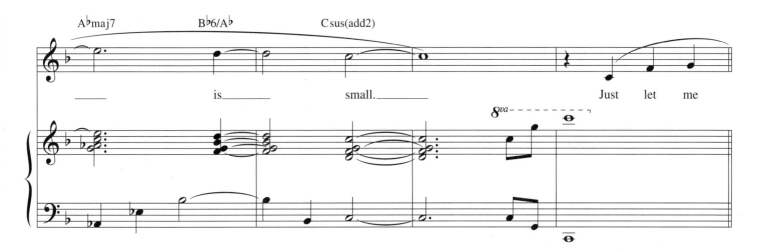

___ is___ small.___ Just let me

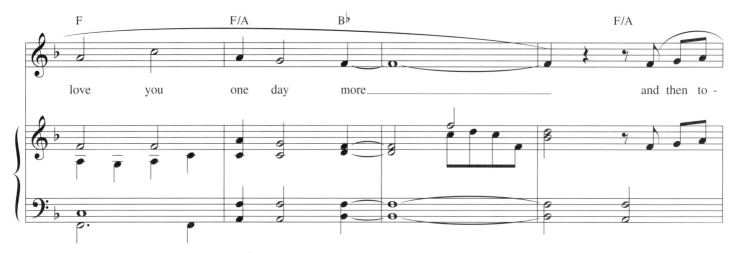

love you one day more_____ and then to-

mor - row night____ when the stars shine__ bright____ I know__

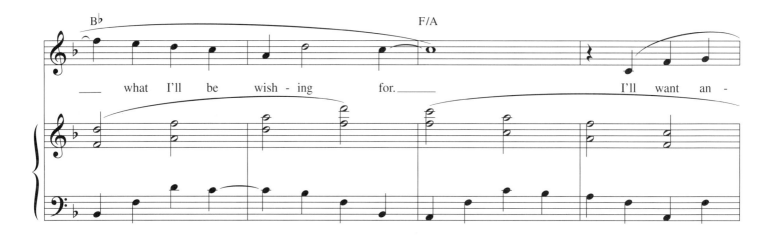

____ what I'll be wish - ing for._____ I'll want an -

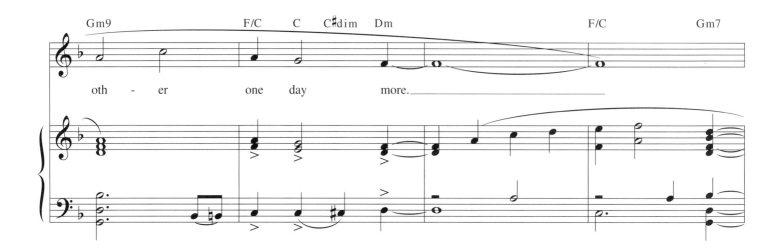

oth - er one day more._____

That's all I'll ask you for.____

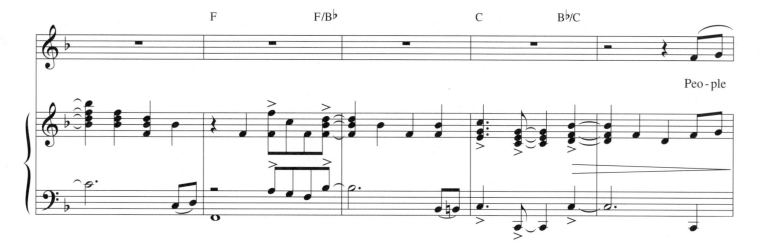

Peo - ple

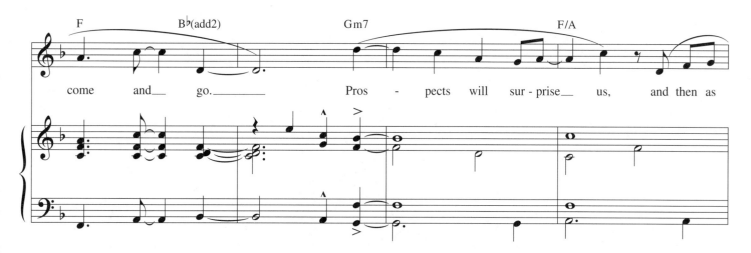

come and__ go._____ Pros - pects will sur - prise__ us, and then as

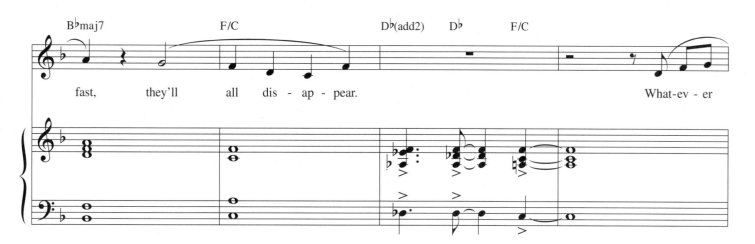

fast, they'll all dis - ap - pear. What-ev - er

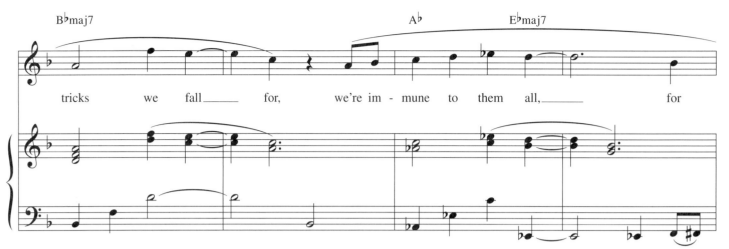

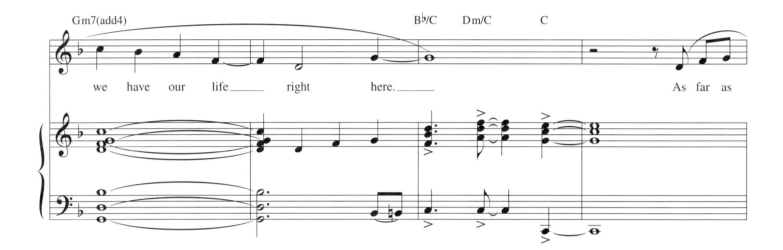

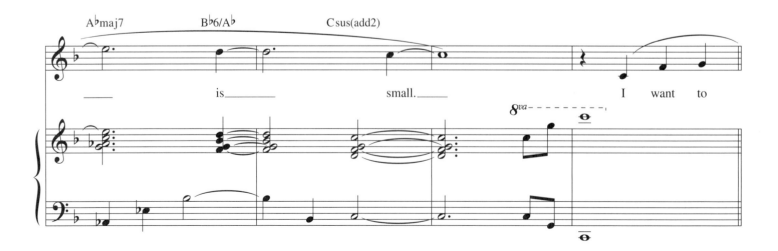

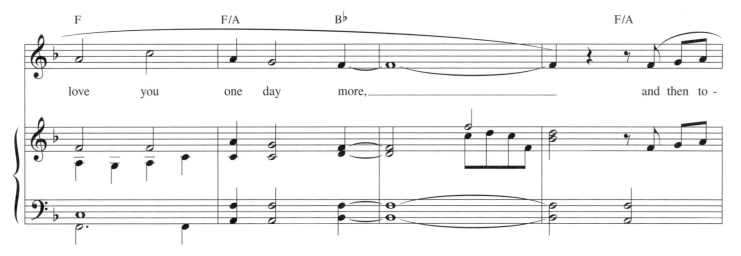

love you one day more,_____ and then to-

mor - row night,____ when the stars shine____ bright,____ I know____

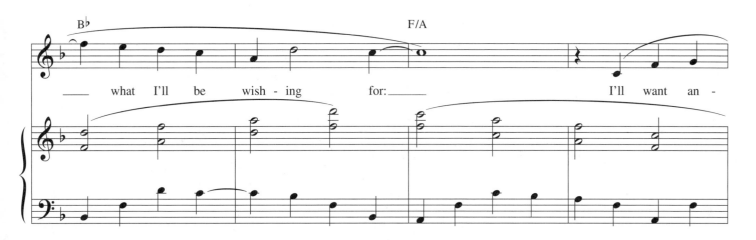

____ what I'll be wish - ing for:_____ I'll want an -

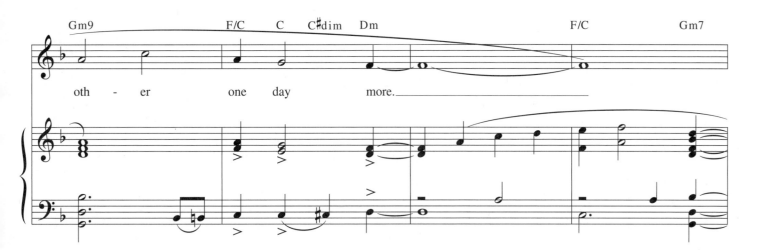

oth - er one day more._____

mor - row night,_____ when the stars shine_____ bright,_____

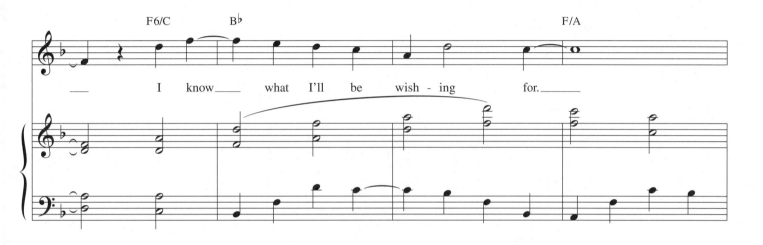

_____ I know_____ what I'll be wish - ing for._____

I'll want an - oth - er, and an - oth - er, and an - oth - er, and an -

cresc. poco a poco

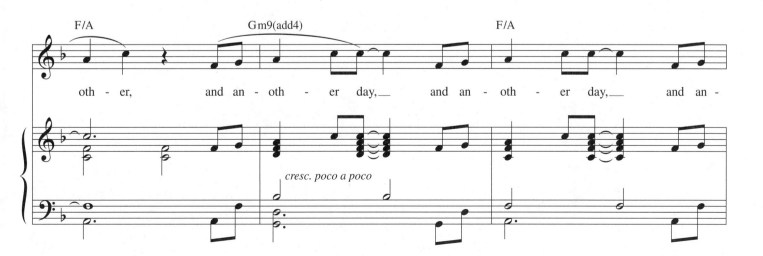

oth - er, and an - oth - er day,___ and an - oth - er day,___ and an -

cresc. poco a poco

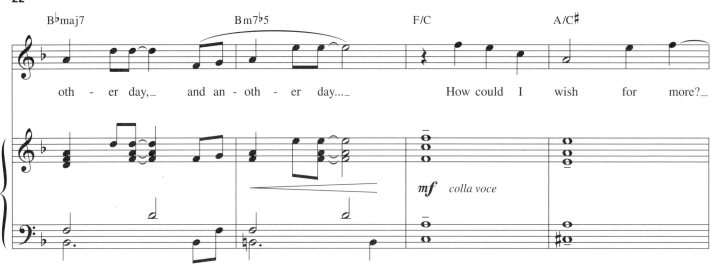

oth - er day,_ and an - oth - er day..._ How could I wish for more?_

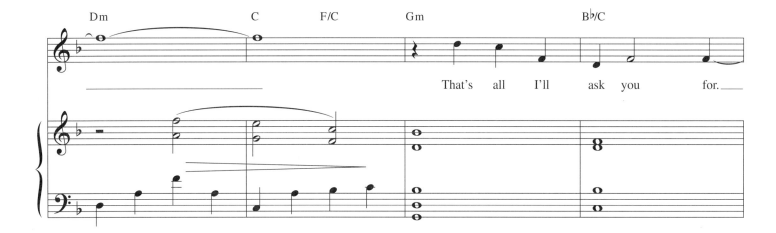

That's all I'll ask you for.___

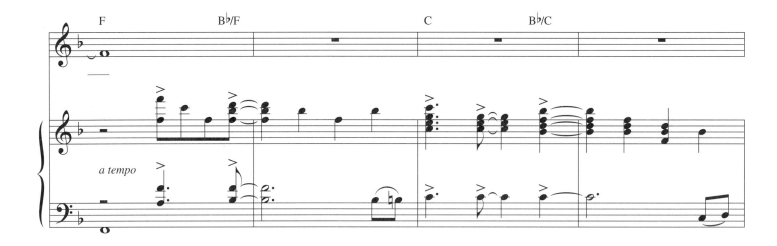

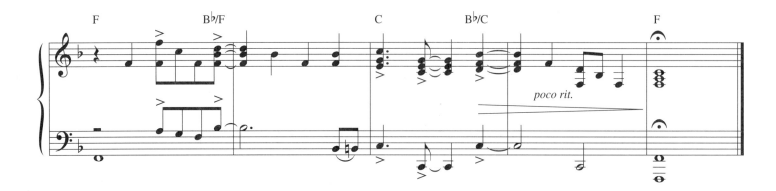

BIG WINGS

Music and Lyrics by
GEORGIA STITT

With energy ♩ = 108

Twelve miles north of Mis - sis-sip - pi.

Noth-in' but cot - ton and road___ out - side of my win - dow.___

The sun beats down___ and the air is dry.___ I think of him___ as the clouds roll by___ and I watch the air-planes o-ver-head.___ And my soul feels___

___ dead.

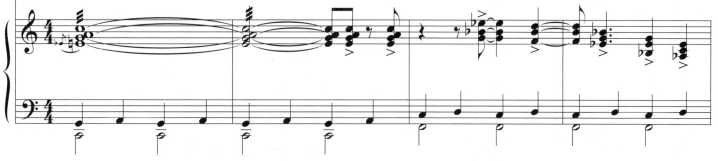

Three or four weeks be - tween_ each vis - it.

A phone call each morn-in' say - in', "Hon,_ it won't be that long."

I try to fake_ that I'm strong and tough,_ but I can't get

to him soon e - nough._____ And a - gain those air -

- planes zoom right by._____ But where the hell__ am I?__

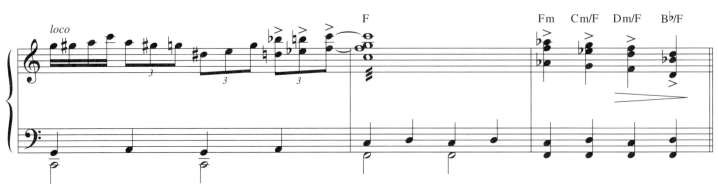

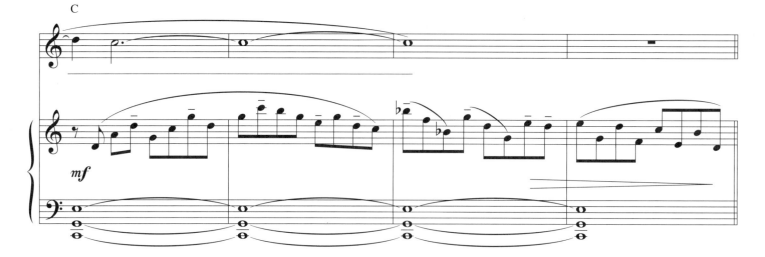

C

Am7   D7/A

All I ev - er want - ed was_ to keep mov - ing._____

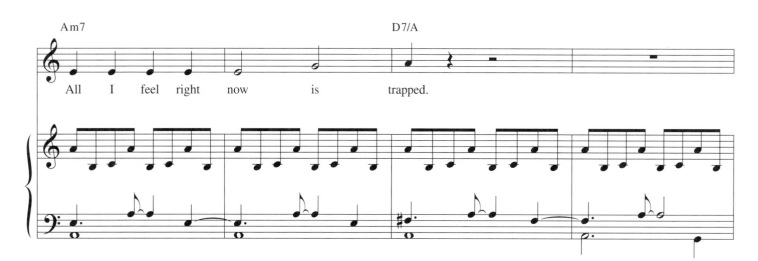

Am7   D7/A

All I feel right now is trapped.

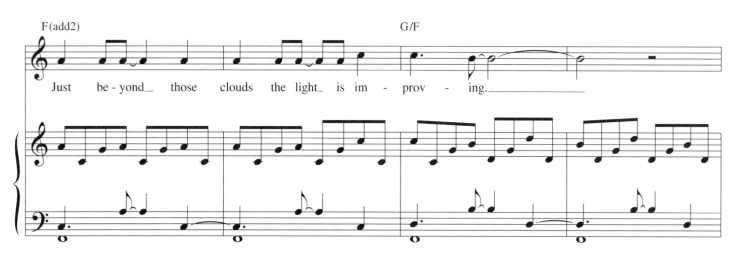

F(add2)   G/F

Just be - yond_ those clouds the light_ is im - prov - ing._____

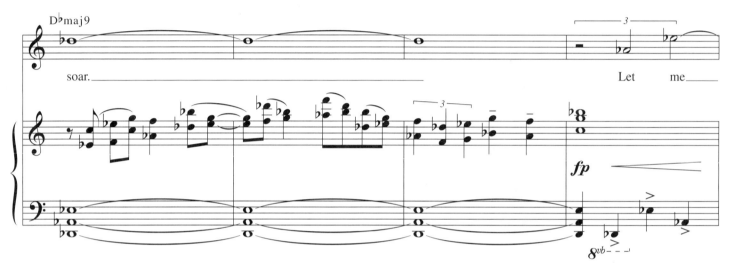

I LAY MY ARMOR DOWN

Music by GEORGIA STITT
Lyrics by FAYE GREENBERG

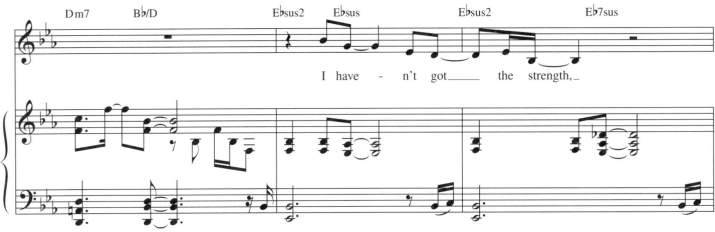

I'd fall on my knees and pray. But here I stand. No God on hand.

I lay my ar - mor down.

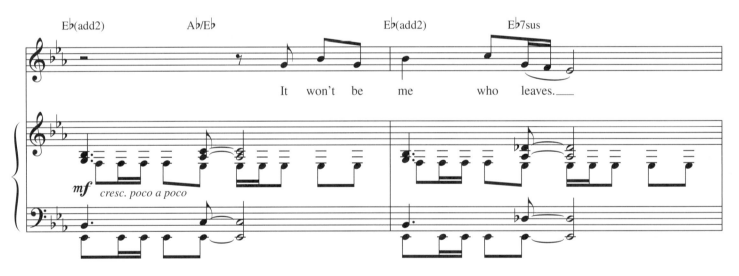

It won't be me who leaves.

No, I won't turn a - way. Do what you will.

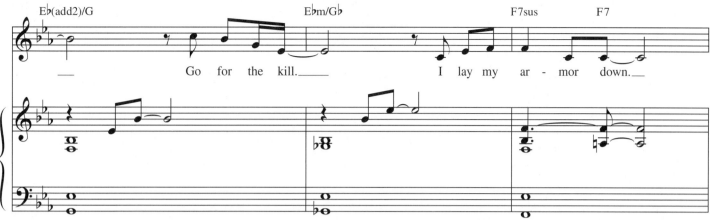

Go for the kill.___ I lay my ar - mor down.___

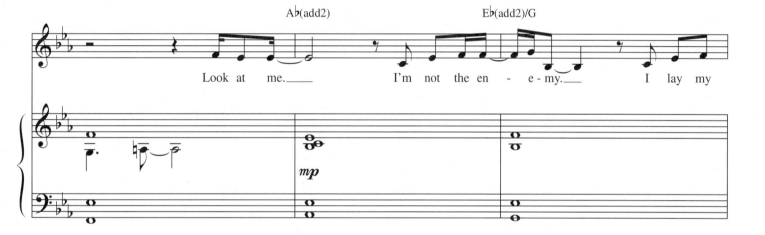

Look at me.___ I'm not the en - e - my.___ I lay my

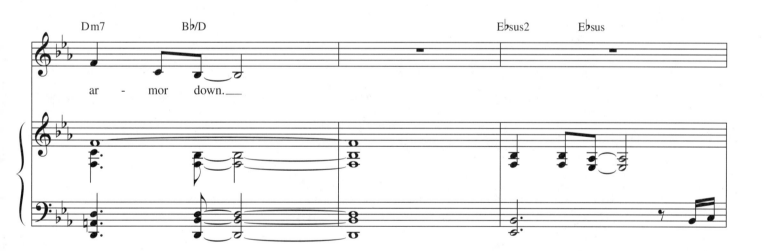

ar - mor down.___

SHE

Music and Lyrics by
GEORGIA STITT

Gentle but steady ♩ = 112

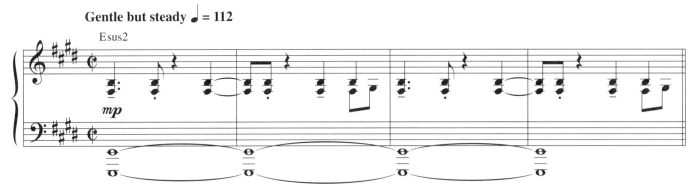

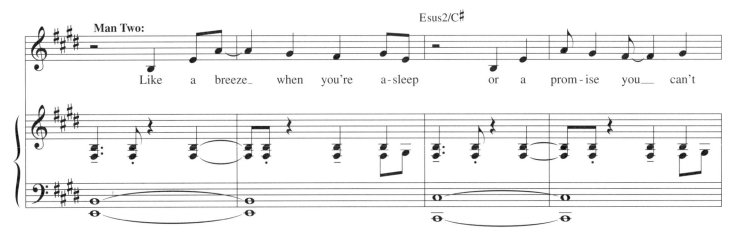

Man Two:
Like a breeze_ when you're a-sleep or a prom-ise you_ can't

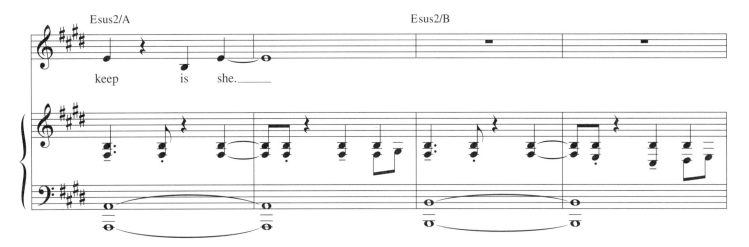

keep is she.___

Man One:
Like De - cem - ber on___ the beach, al - ways just be - yond___ your

reach   is   she._____   You   want   to

You   want   to

claim   her   all_____   for   your   own,_____   but   if   you

claim   her   all_____   for   your   own,_____

cling   too   hard,_____   you'll   find   that   you   are   left   a -

Lyrics:
is she._____ She grabs your

hand and charg - es a - head,   and if you
She charg - es a - head.___

stall, an - oth - er man might win her heart in -

D/C   C(add2)   D/C   Bm/C   D/C   Cmaj7

stead._____

B   E/B   B/C♯   C♯m7

Man Two:

But re-mem - ber what she needs.__ Like a rose a-mid__ the

Asus2   B7sus   Esus2

weeds_____ is she.

A(add2)   B/A

Give_____ her room._____

Give_____ her room._____

mf

Let_____ her roam._____

Let_____ her roam.

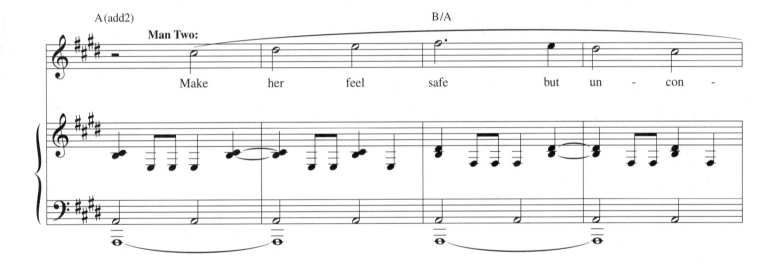

Man Two:
Make her feel safe but un - con -

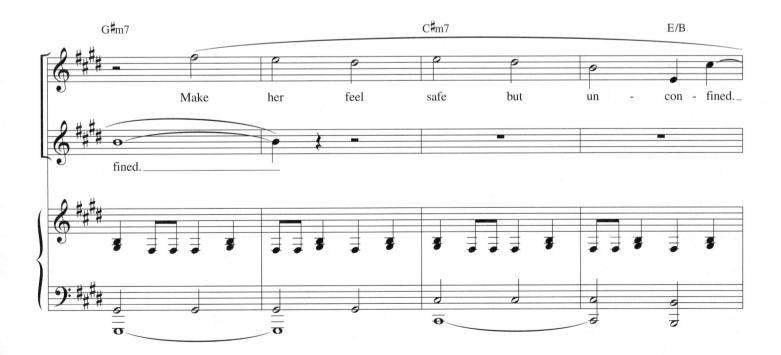

Make her feel safe but un - con - fined.___

fined._____

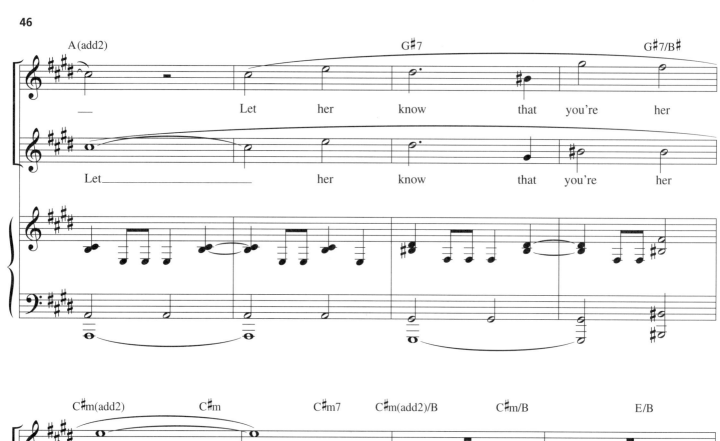

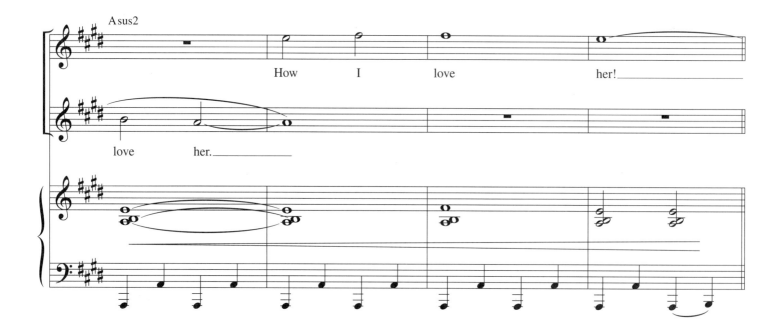

for - ev - er, now, _____ is

now, _____ is

she. _____

she. _____

LIFE IS NOT A CAMERA

Music and Lyrics by
GEORGIA STITT

Gently, like a reflecting pool ♩ = 108

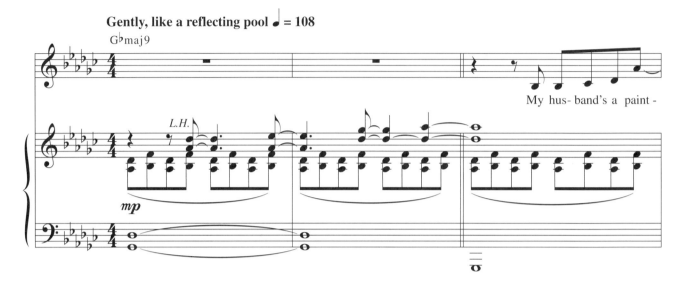

My hus- band's a paint -

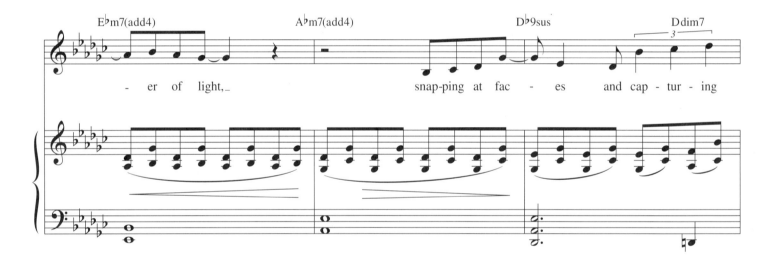

- er of light,_ snap-ping at fac - es and cap - tur - ing

souls_____ in black and white. He sees the whole world_____ through a

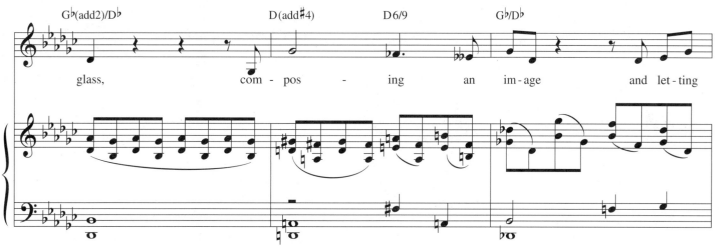

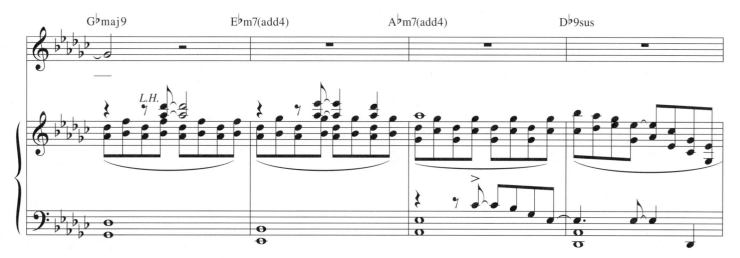

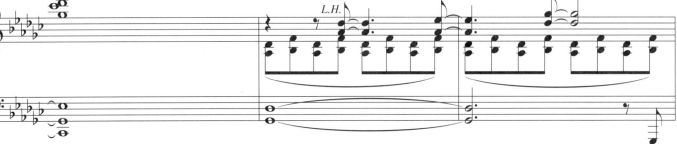

Tempo I

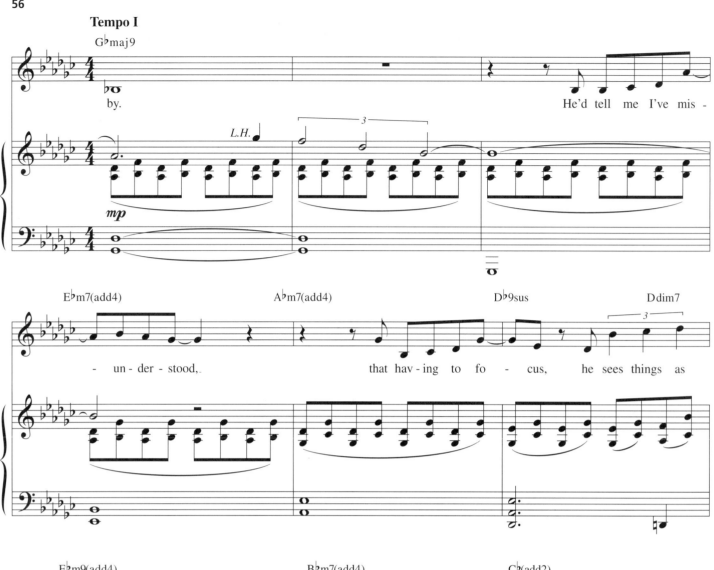

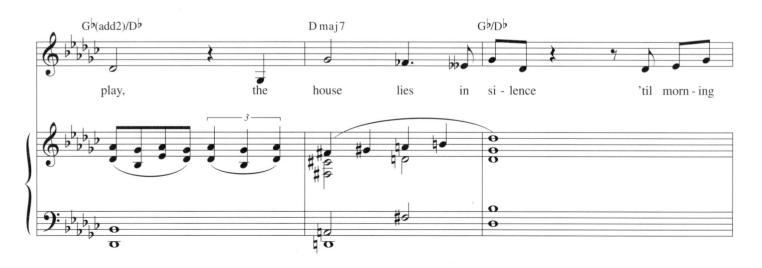

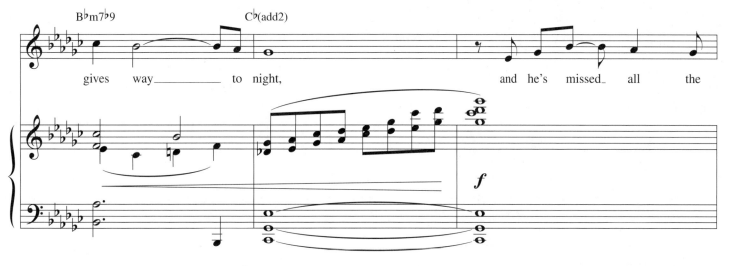

gives way_____ to night, and he's missed_ all the

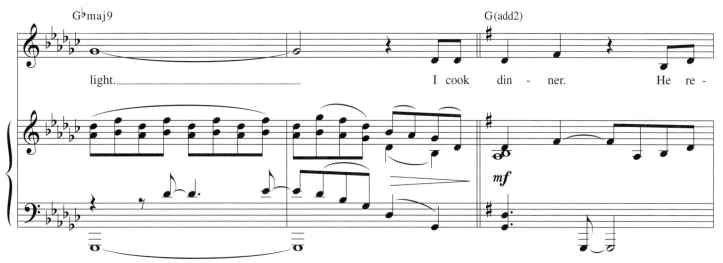

light._____ I cook din - ner. He re -

heats it, and he's sur-prised that it___ got cold. He swears to - mor - row___

___ he'll eat____ with his wife._____ But first he shows me the most

THESE TWO

for Jason Robert Brown

Music by GEORGIA STITT
Lyrics by HOWARD SCHWARTZ

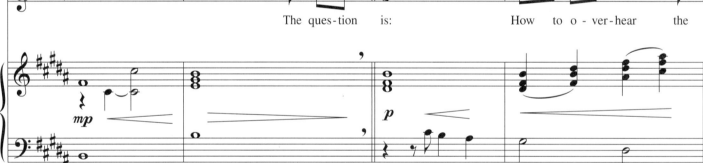

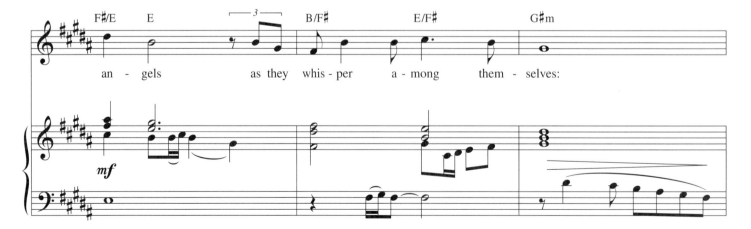

twin stars, _____ shall meet and be

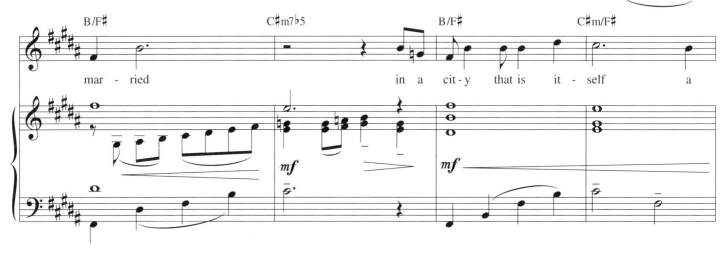

mar - ried in a cit - y that is it - self a

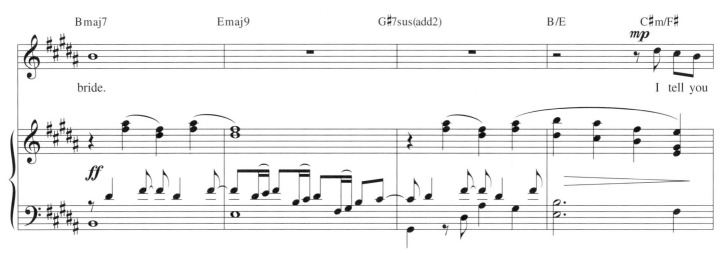

bride. I tell you

I have heard them, and I have heard the spir - its of sons and

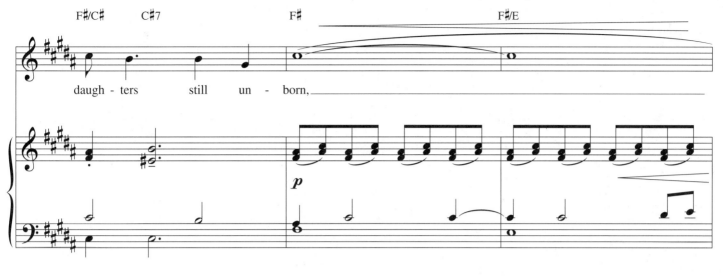

daugh - ters still un - born,_____

beg - ging me to take care,_____

take care that the nest does not burn down._____

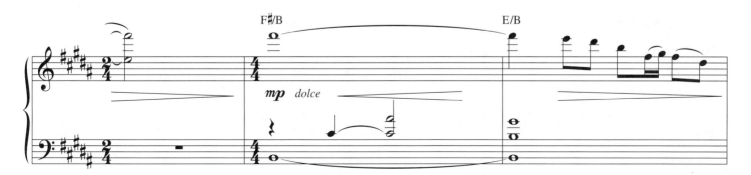

I GET TO SHOW YOU THE OCEAN

for MCB on her first birthday

Music and Lyrics by
GEORGIA STITT

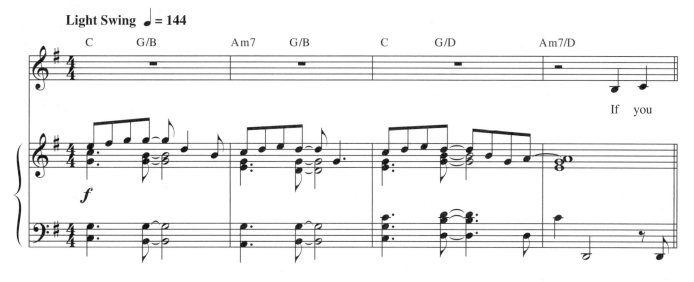

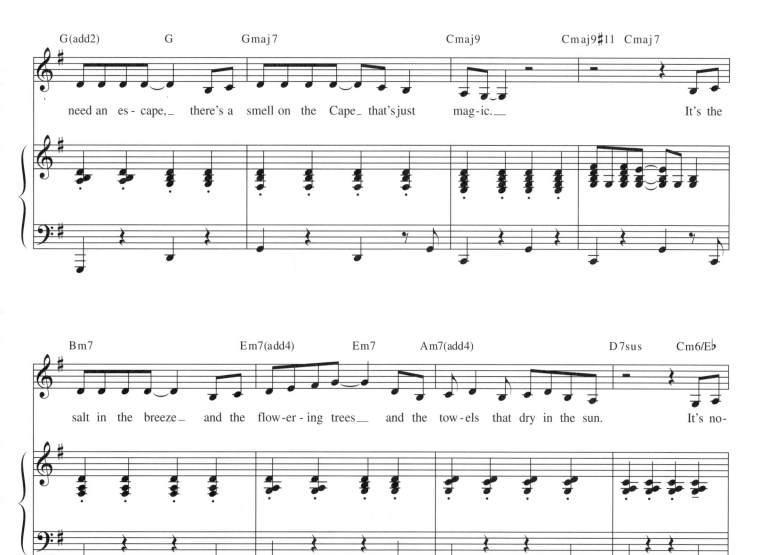

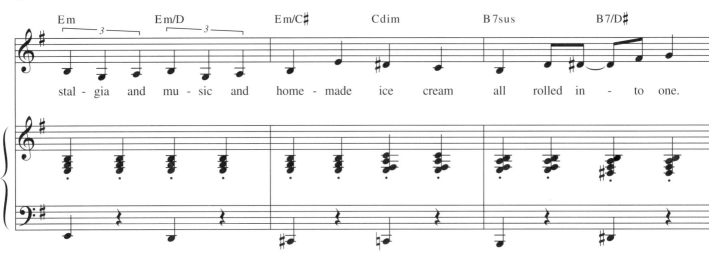

stal - gia and mu - sic and home - made ice cream all rolled in - to one.

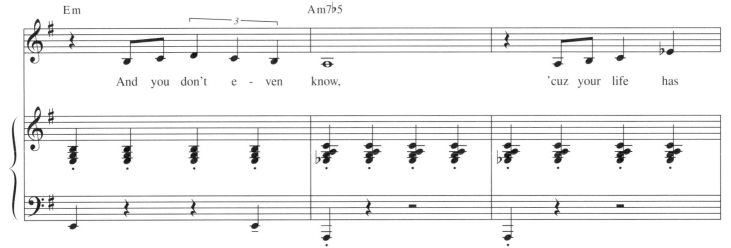

And you don't e - ven know, 'cuz your life has

just be - gun. But, I'm gon - na show_

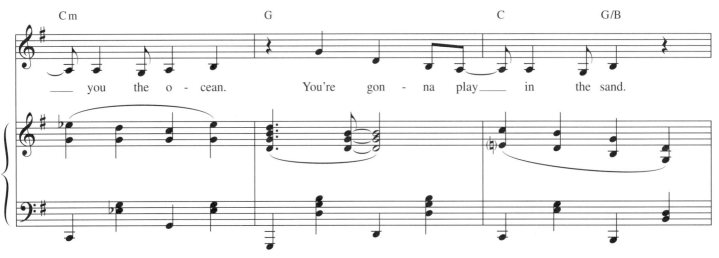

___ you the o - cean. You're gon - na play___ in the sand.

And when sum-mer is through, __ there's a lot we can do__ in the win - ter.__ You'll have snow-flakes to catch.__ We'll make cook-ies from scratch.__ Get a par-rot and teach him to sing. Who could guess that so quick-ly I'm filled with joy that on - ly you__ can bring?

IT ALMOST FELT LIKE LOVE

Music and Lyrics by
GEORGIA STITT

Steady, with a hard groove ♩ = 96

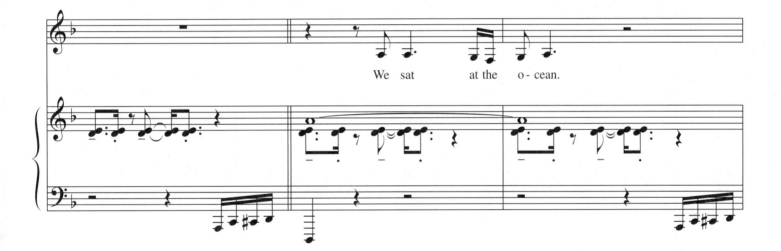

We sat at the o - cean.

We talked in the dark. The wind____ made it

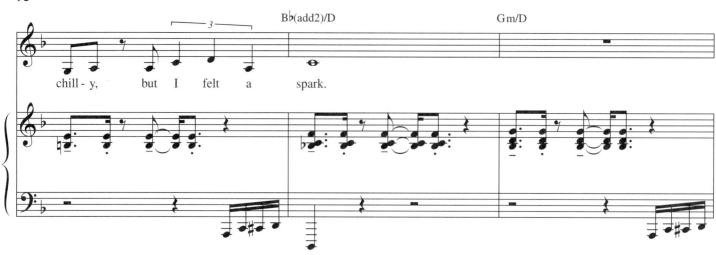

chill - y, but I felt a spark.

The night was-n't per-fect. These things nev-er

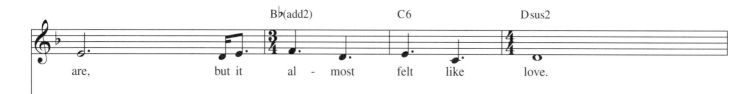

are, but it al - most felt like love.

You laughed and I flirt-ed. We walked hand in

hand. My hair____ was a mess, all en-tan-gled with

sand. It was - n't ro-man-tic.

Not a moon, nor a star, but it al - most felt like

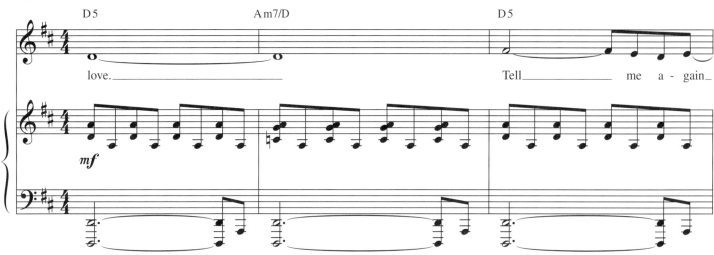

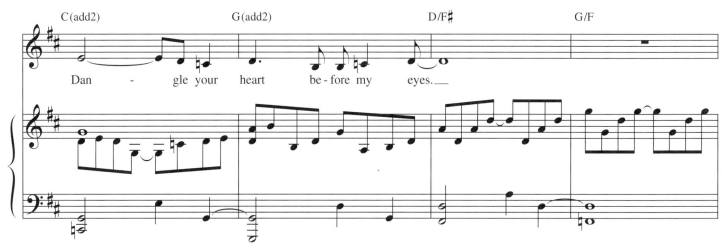

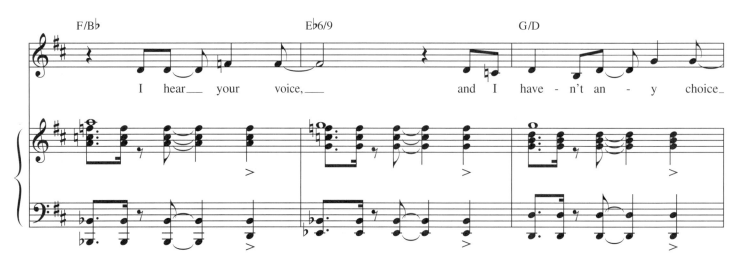

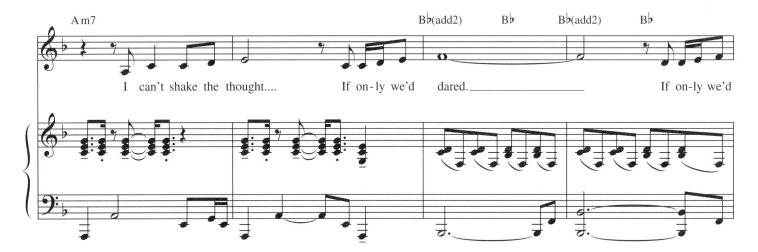

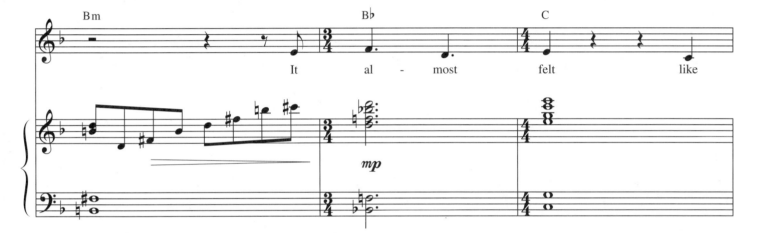

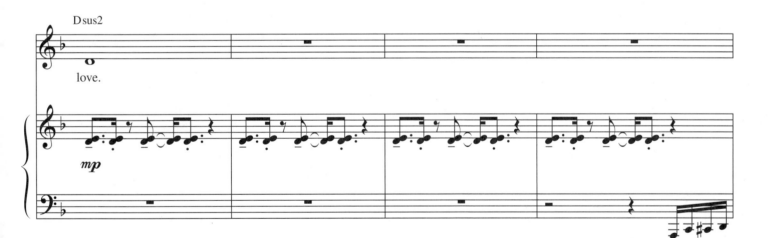

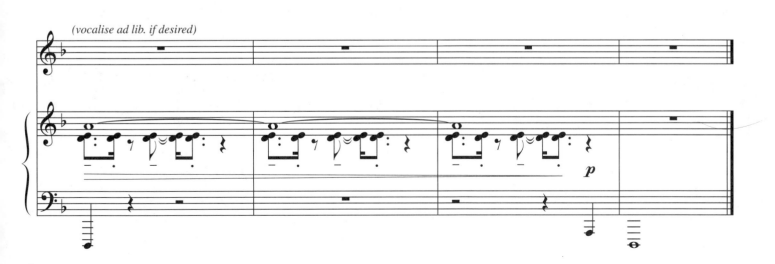

AIR

Music by SAM DAVIS
Lyrics by GEORGIA STITT

Driving and passionate (not too fast!) ♩ = 85

* *Recorded one half step lower*

G(add2)   **C(add2)/G**   **D 7**

That which is found＿ must once＿ have been lost.   If there's a wall,＿ it takes work＿ to move＿ it.

B♭maj7   **D/A**

Here comes a chance,＿ and I'm lung - ing for - ward,   mak-ing a vow＿ that I will＿ not fail.＿

B♭maj7   **D/A**

Thou-sands of men＿ have ap - proached＿ this point＿ with - out ev - er ven - tur-ing to＿ in - hale＿

E(add2)/D   **B(add2)**

＿   air.＿

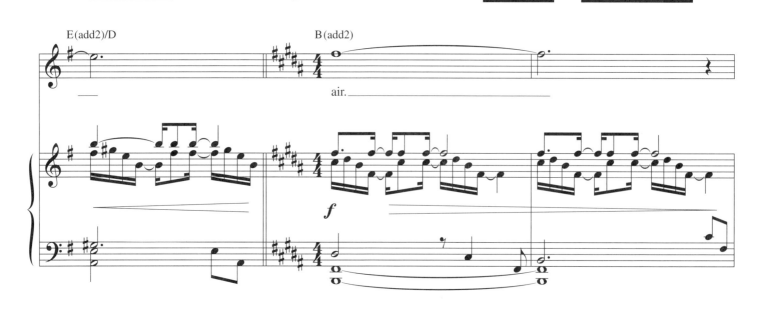

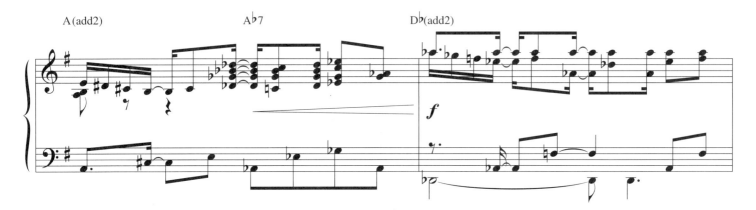

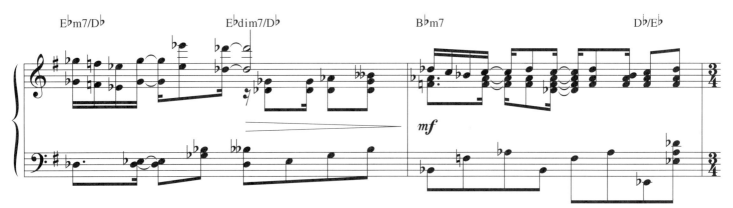

PERFECT SUMMER

Music by SAM DAVIS
Lyrics by GEORGIA STITT

THIS ORDINARY THURSDAY

Music and Lyrics by
GEORGIA STITT

Funky, rhythmic

Most days by now_____ I have run all my er- rands. I have

read all my e-mail. I have talked on the phone.___

Most days by now_____ I have dealt with the laun - dry. I have_

nuked up my din-ner, and I've done it a-lone.

Most nights I catch my-self gaz - ing through cur-tains in-to

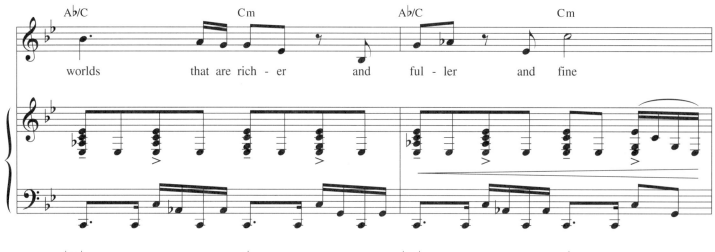

worlds that are rich - er and ful - ler and fine

But to-night, for once, the rich - es are

mine!_____ All

mine! So I will

Tempo I

raise all the shades,__ and then I'll fill the room__ with can - dles.

Let them see what they will! We'll just

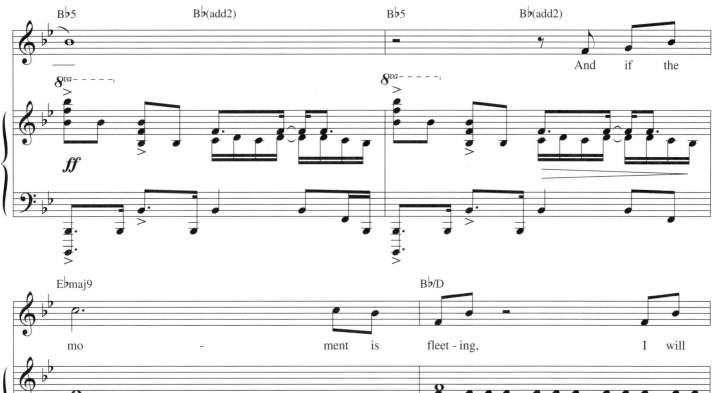

mo - ment is fleet - ing, I will

save what I can. I can

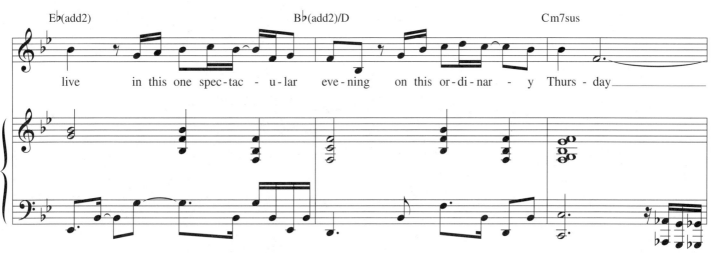

live in this one spec - tac - u - lar eve - ning on this or - di - nar - y Thurs - day